In memory of the Radium Girls

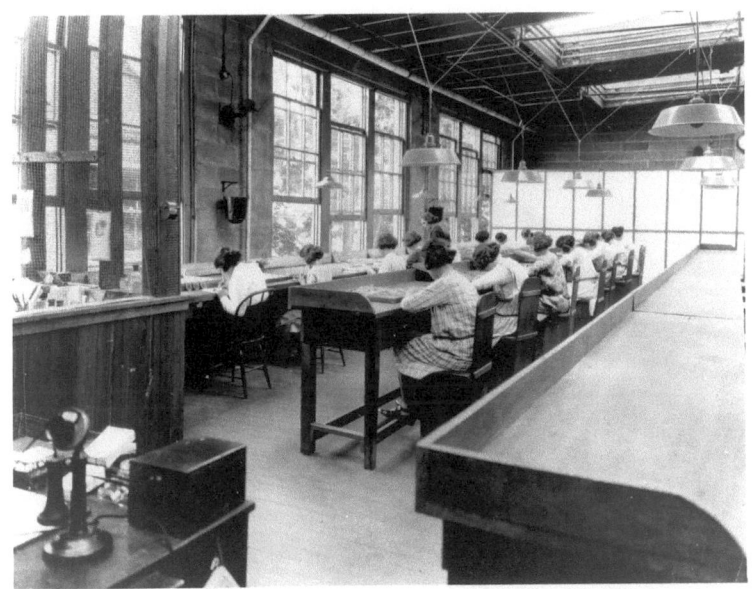

The Radium Girls, workers at the factory of the
US Radium Corporation

Thomas M. Meine

VINTAGE WATCHES
RADIUM AND TRITIUM
Luminous paint on dial and hands

With special thanks to Luigi Gori for making available images of lumed vintage watches from his collection.

Bibliographic information published by the Deutsche Nationalbibliothek:

The Deutsche Nationalbibliothek lists this publication in the
Deutsche Nationalbibliografie; detailed bibliographic data
are available on the Internet at http://dnb.dnb.de

Printed and published by
BoD - Books on Demand, Norderstedt
All rights reserved

Copyright © Thomas M. Meine

September 2021 (5th edition)

ISBN 9 783752 821406

CONTENTS   Page

1921 magazine ad for 'UNDARK', a product of the
Radium Luminous Material Corporation
(later U.S. Radium Corporation)

INTRODUCTION

Radium (radium 226) and Tritium contained as activators in luminous paint on watch dials (numbers, markers, dots) and hands, besides other radioactive materials, are subject to never ending discussions amongst vintage watch collectors, especially those, who are looking for lumed timepieces from earlier periods.

Opinions differ in what concerns eventual health risks, not only amongst the watch collectors but also between the professionals. Many ask themselves why those watches should still pose a threat to human health, whilst the 'glow' is long gone. True, the glow is gone – but not the radium (or many other radioactive substances used as activators, as well as other elements following down the decay chain, with some difference explained later).

This book intends to give *a general overview* of radium- and tritium issues for the *vintage watch collector* interested in this subject. It is in no way addressing the physicists, chemists, or nuclear scientists and will not go far beyond the necessary for a basic understanding. There will also be no statements about how much any measured values are affecting human health. This depends on too many factors and the topic is anyhow subject to controversial discussions.

Overall, it is a matter of high complexity and not as trivial as often presumed. The various issues are usually dealt with in a variety of shorter, specialized articles.

Any deeper interest must be referred to professional documentation, whereby this book will hopefully help to look in the right direction, already with a basic understanding.

In short: All of this is a more general treatise for the watch collector, also due to the fact, that the author is not in a position to contribute something of added value for the scientists in this field. This would furthermore involve detailed information, which is 90% outside the core topic, with the inevitable result, that non-experts could soon no longer see the wood for the trees. Indeed, anything above the pure essentials would require in-depth studies in that field to fully understand such a complex and multidisciplinary matter. Radioactive decay processes and their effects are related to the work of physicists, chemists, biochemists, or in the area of medicine.

The overall intention was therefore to produce documentation that elevates itself somewhat above a meager statement like: *'Luminous paint on watch dials and hands containing radium or tritium can be dangerous to some extent, especially when substances get inside the body, but all is relative and subject to different opinions'.*

On the other hand, it should – whenever possible – stay below a level where humble people would say: *'When most of a content is useless for a general understanding, things are called scientific'.*

Nevertheless, some issues have, up to a certain degree, been dealt with in more detail. This is certainly not enough to prepare some watch collectors to take the mike on a scientific panel dealing with radioactivity but should provide sufficient information to understand *'what's happening and why'* and to make one's own assessment about any possible dangers to health.

When talking about threats from luminous paint on watch dials and hands containing radium, tritium (or other elements) as activators, one must distinguish between the pure collecting and/or wearing of such a watch, and collectors, who are also opening it up for whatever purpose, be it just to have a look at the movement or doing cleaning-, restoration- or repair jobs, especially if the dial is laid bare in the process. Things are also of vital importance in the process of professional servicing, -repair, or -restoration.

The dangers arising from the application of luminous paint containing radioactive substances during the *original production process* are a matter of the past, as the new luminous products do not contain any radium, tritium, or other radioactive elements anymore (or are, in the case of the use of tritium, kept in closed tubes).

It is not primarily the radioactive radiation and their influence from *outside* our body we have to be afraid of today, but the fact, that the harmful substances – gases or scattered particles – can get into the body by inhaling (respiratory passages) or by digestion (through the esophagus into the digestive system) and from there also into the blood.

Radium and tritium are not the only harmful, originally applied elements, which can be found on vintage watch dials and hands. I have, however, largely restricted myself to these elements, as they represent by far the largest part. Others are, for instance, promethium or strontium. The latter, because of its special danger, has been shortly dealt with in a separate chapter.

What concerns the different types of timepieces, the problem can mostly be found on lumed wristwatches from the early beginnings and up to the 1980s or occasionally even beyond. The more dangerous radium should only very rarely appear on watches after 1960.

Pocket watches are of course also affected, whilst they were already more and more becoming obsolete at the time of radium and later tritium as an activator for the luminous paint. If still produced as mass products in those periods – mostly until the time of the application of radium, we can often see a heavy application of this material. The size of the dial, well readable at night when lumed, often secured them a prominent place at the bedside table. This type of use, like with wristwatches frequently used in dim or dark environments, often triggered an over-rich re-painting after some time. And, of course, some clocks have similar problems.

Collectors storing radium lumed watches, especially from the 1920s to the 1960s, in unventilated areas in the house, could be exposed to dangerous doses of easily inhaled radon gas (radon 222). Recently, scientists tested a collection of radium-dial watches, which had produced radon gas concentrations far above safe levels. See more details in the chapter 'radon issues' on page 54.

In any case, studies concerning the dangers originating from radium lumed watches have substantially increased in recent times, with a clear tendency towards conclusions expressing a lot more concern than in the past (justified or not). We can also find special research work based on 'real' watches and collections, with in-depth measurements of radiation, types and amounts, effects on health, and not solely in theory.

Pocket watches are usually carried near the hips, often with the dial facing the body, with no shielding by the case, unlike with wristwatches, where the dial is facing away from the body (arm). The shielding by the case ensures much better protection. An exception are the wristwatches in plastic cases, but this is a generation of timepieces possibly dealing with tritium and not with radium anymore.

LUMINOUS PAINT IN THE WATCH INDUSTRY

Above: Junghans wristwatch from the 1950s. Radium lumed numbers and hands. The luminous paint was undergoing strong decomposition in line with aging. The dial is burned to a brownish color. The crystal has been replaced due to damage by radioactive radiation. A very strong indication of radioactive radiation measured with a Geiger counter (see measured values later).

A watch is a nice thing to have, it tells you the time and possibly other things, provided there is enough light around. But what, if you are in low- or no light conditions?

It's an old problem and a variety of methods and substances have been used and tested to bring luminescence onto dial and hands. The first solutions go back to the early 1900s. During WWI and thereafter, the military was the driving force for watches where the time could be checked also at night and in dark environments, directly from the watch itself. The same applies to various instruments e.g. used in submarines or airplanes. For this reason, a luminous material had to be developed to make the numbers and indications on the dial and the hands 'glow' by themselves.

Basically, all materials can be brought to glow when they are heated up enough, but only a few substances can have a *'cold light emission'*, which is the ability to absorb energy in various forms and to transform it into visible light. Atoms and molecules are activated and when returning to the initial (basic-) state, the difference in energy is emitted in form of light. This effect is called luminescence.

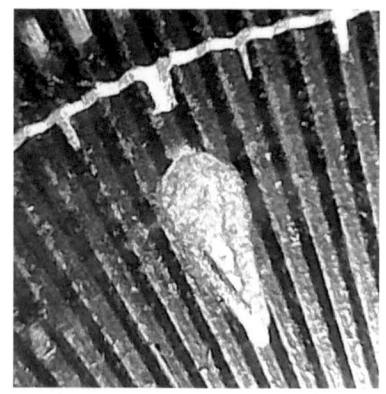
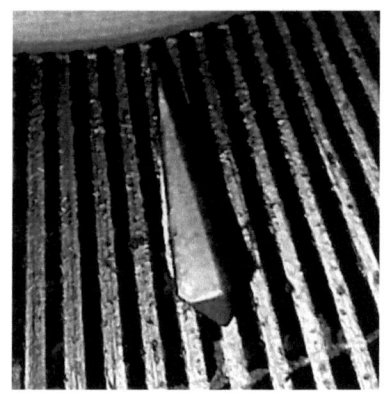

Top left: most of the luminous paint is still on the marker, but a substantial part has already fallen off.

Top right: the luminous paint is completely gone from the marker except for a small remnant on the left.

Left: Also here, the luminous paint is completely gone from the number, except for a small remnant.

It is obvious, that the loose particles are all over the dial, crystal and watch, unless they have fallen out at some place before when the watch was opened.

The development of luminous paint on watches

Radium

At first, the activation of the luminous substance was affected by radium, or its isotope radium 226 to be precise. This began during WWI and ended in the 1960s. Radium 226 has a half-life period of 1.600 years. Occasionally, also strontium and promethium had been used.

All of this has been completely stopped, primarily due to the health risks in the production process.

As these watches are still massively around, the risk is now with all people owning such a timepiece, especially if they are opening the watch or are even working on it.

The wearer of such a watch can be fairly relaxed but should pay the necessary respect. Wearing a radium lumed watch with the crystal down (especially an acrylic one), as some contemporaries do it to 'protect' it, mostly with a flex band attached to the case, might not be the best idea. More detailed information will be found in the chapter 'The activators – radium, tritium and others', page 22.

Tritium

In the 1960s and up until the 1990s, the more harmless tritium has replaced the radium 226 as an activator. Tritium has a lot lower energy and a half-life period of only 12.3 years (and decays at this rate thereafter). The health risks are substantially reduced, as long as the watch is not opened.

Tritium, a radioactive isotope of hydrogen, decomposes into the stable helium isotope ^{3}H. It emits electrons along with its beta-decay, which interact with the phosphorous material. The luminous effect is fading much sooner compared to radium-lumed watches (half-life period of 12.3 years compared to 1,600 years of radium 226), with the light source becoming too dim with a *useful* end after 25 to 30 years.

In any case, this always goes along with the degradation of the phosphorous stuff itself, reducing the brightness and the overall effectiveness also for this reason.

Combined with the fact, that tritium is an expensive material (often more expensive than the rest of a cheaper type watch) and producers have used as little as possible, we can often see an effective period of only 10 to 20 years.

GTLS Tritium H3 (new development)

To further limit the dangers of tritium, the GTLS (Gaseous Tritium Light Source) has been developed. In colloquial speech and referring to the illumination of watch dials, we talk more about H3-watches or Tritium H3-watches, instead of GTLS.

The tritium is put into closed tubes, made of borosilicate glass, which is coated on the inside with a phosphorous layer.

The product is known under the brand names 'Trigalight' and 'Betalight', made by the Swiss company mb-microtec. Already invented in the 1960s, it causes a glow a lot stronger than what came from the previous luminous paints containing tritium. Colors: green, orange, yellow, ice blue, red, and pink.

This product did not only find its way onto watch dials but can be seen in emergency lighting, key pendants or other 'glow-in-the-dark' products and is also used by the military.

Intact GTLS are completely shielding off the beta-emissions of tritium. However, the sudden deceleration of the electrons causes a so-called 'Bremsstrahlung' (the original German term is commonly used, the translation would be 'breaking radiation') in the X-ray range, which can penetrate to the outside. GTLS with a high amount of tritium can increase the overall radiation burden.

The GTLS used in watches produces a light, which is not enough to be recognized in daylight but can well be seen in the dark. The tubes range from tiny, small enough the fit on the dial and hands, to the ones, which have the size of a pencil in other applications.

The producers guarantee a lifetime of minimum 10 years

Dangers: When the tube is damaged and tritium is leaking, there is a (limited) danger for humans or the environment. It could eventually be inhaled and then continues to emit beta-radiation inside the human body.

A particular danger is the biological activity of tritium, which means it can, like hydrogen, get into the cycle of materials. As a part of radioactively polluted drinking water, it might cause some harm. This is, however, not seen as a great danger.

New, non-radioactive luminescent paint

In the context of this book, dealing with the dangers of luminous paint containing radium or tritium, we could end the listing at this stage, but for the sake of completeness, the modern materials, applied today, shall also be mentioned:

Both radium and tritium were finally done away with in favor of non-radioactive and harmless substances like **LumiNova** or **Super-LumiNova**. Tritium is still around, where the dangers have been overcome by the use in GTLS, as described before. Super-LumiNova is a further development of LumiNova, with an increased luminosity in the colors yellowish-green, bluish-green and violet-blue.

The pigments were developed by the Japanese company Nemoto & Co. Ltd. The Swiss company RC Tritec is producing this luminescent paint since 2007 under license from Nemoto as an 'All Swiss' product. It is the luminous paint used by almost all European watch producers and others worldwide. The pigments are so-called 'afterglow pigments'.

Super-LumiNova has a very strong light, which, however, must be repeatedly charged by a light source. The luminous effect is soon fading, but should, in most cases, 'make it through the night'.

LumiNova and Super-LumiNova fall into the category of photoluminescent lumes. They glow very bright after exposure to light and fade slowly after time, enough to read the watch in the dark for some hours. The pigments glow through inorganic phosphorescence. Stimulated by sufficient day- or artificial light, the electrons are brought to a higher energy level and are then releasing the energy difference in the form of visible light. When the energy slows down, the brightness slows down, until the photoluminescent material is charged again.

The longer and more intense the exposure to light, the more complete the stimulation up to total saturation, the stronger the glow and its duration, up to the end of the night.

What concerns the lifetime of the pigments of Super-LumiNova, it can be assumed that it can theoretically be 'charged' infinitely with a more or less stable luminosity. Although a reduction of the luminous intensity (brightness) is occurring, it is a process spread over a very long time and can often hardly be noticed.

The luminous pigments are not influenced by the charging and discharging, so their use is guaranteed for long.

What concerns the colors, there is practically no limit to the variations. Green is however the most suitable choice, as the human eye has its highest sensitivity in this wavelength range. Orange is also well visible for the eye, whilst under water – for diver's watches – blue is preferred.

Besides this, some major producers had come out with their own products, like Rolex, where 'Chromalight' can be found on their Deepsea watches.

Just shortly mentioned here: When the watches with LCD display came out with batteries inside, the problem was solved by giving the dial a background light at the push of a button (of course reducing the life of the battery).

LUMINESCENCE
FLUORESCENCE and PHOSPHORESCENCE

Luminescence

Luminescence is the glowing of a substance (emission of light) under influence of energy not resulting from heat (= 'cold light emission' – e.g. chemical, electrical or mechanical influence), as opposed to an effect caused by temperature (incandescence). In terms of the duration, we distinguish between 'fluorescence' and 'phosphorescence'.

A. Fluorescence

Fluorescence is a spontaneous emission of light and only of very short duration (less than 1/1000 of a second). There is no storage ability.

Occasionally, safety vests or other high-visibility clothing, as well as specific traffic signs, are referred to as examples. That is, however, not correct, as they are 'only' reflective materials, which shine a light back to their source. Here, we have no form of energy transformation at all.

B. Phosporescence

The phosphorescence has a longer durability (1/1000 of a second at least, but can also last up to a few hours). This is based on the storage of energized electrons (storage ability).

A bit confusing: The chemical element phosphorus (P, 15), named for its light-emitting ability, is emitting this light not by phosphorescence, but through chemiluminescence.

Whatever, especially the fluorescence, but also the phosphorescence are not ideal solutions. There has to be a way to make this glowing permanent at all times.

This can for instance be reached, by mixing luminous material with an activator (**reaction to radioactive material**), which is permanently inciting it to glow.

In general, we distinguish between:

chemoluminescence (based on a chemical reaction),

photoluminescence (reaction to daylight or UV-light,

electroluminescence (reaction to electrical energy),

radioluminescence **(reaction to radioactive material)**, in the case of the lumed watch dials and hands,

The substance mostly used in glow-in-the-dark products and watch dials and hands, in combination with radium and tritium, is **zinc sulfide**. It is luminescent, category phosphorescent (strong).

ZINC SULFIDE

Zinc sulfide – is the universal luminescence substance, mostly used on radium- and tritium activated watch dials and hands.

Zinc sulfide (not to be mixed up with sulfite) is an organic compound with the chemical formula of ZnS (zinc and sulfur).

It is created through the oxidation of zinc and sulfur (one of the possible methods, formula: $8Zn + S_8 = 8\ ZnS$).

ZnS exists in two main crystalline forms, sphalerite (most stable) and wurtzite – see molecular models in that order from left to right below – with a very rare variant called polhemusite.

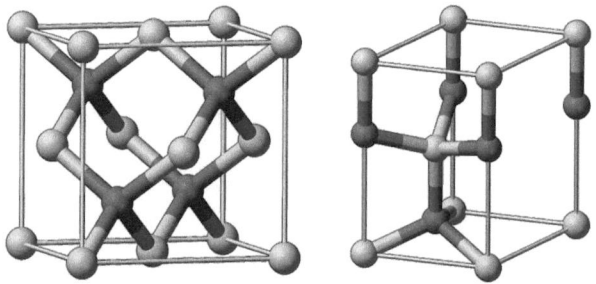

Zinc sulfide can be brought to glow for instance by exposure to light or ultraviolet rays. In this case, however, the glowing effect is soon fading away. Mixing the substance with radium (or tritium), as a permanent activator, results in a permanent glow, meaning that this effect is created by itself without any external source (self-luminescent). It lasts for many years. Note: The glowing is *always* there, you just can't see it in the surrounding daylight.

Zinc sulfide is phosphorescent. It can be mixed with other compounds, to vary the color of the lume.

Besides zinc sulfide, also zinc silicate was occasionally used as a luminous substance, because of the white color it emits. Zinc silicate has a shorter glowing effect and is fluorescent, unlike zinc sulfide, which is phosphorescent. But this does not make any difference, as long as there is a permanent activation through radioactive material.

THE ACTIVATORS – RADIUM, TRITIUM AND OTHERS

To permanently activate the zinc sulfide, it had been mixed with radioactive elements like radium (radium 226) and later with tritium (T or ^{3}H).

Occasionally, also other radioactive substances had been used, but those, because not so often applied, will be neglected in this particular chapter, but dealt with later. In any case, people getting near such a type of luminous paint should also be aware of other radioactive materials.

Such other radioactive elements, which have been seldom applied, are radium 228 (another isotope of Ra, 88), thorium 228 (radiothorium, isotope of thorium Th, 90). Their alpha particles activate the luminescence; their beta particles can however penetrate through the case and cause damages to the wrist of the wearer of watches.

Beginning with the 1950s, also Strontium 90 (an isotope of strontium Sr, 38) had been used. It decays into yttrium 90 (an isotope of yttrium Y, 39) under emission of beta radiation and then to the stable, non-radioactive zirconium 90.

The relating beta radiation is very hard and strong and had caused damage to the wrist, more than other comparable substances. Its use was forbidden for that reason (see separate chapter on strontium 90, ' Strontium – the bone seeker', page 45).

Collectors of vintage wristwatches from that period cannot be sure to be confronted 'only' with radium. It is a special case of danger involving also the wearer of such a watch, who would otherwise be safe, as long as the watch is not opened.

Radium and Tritium – the main difference

The difference between radium and tritium, in view of their use as an activator of luminous substances and the dangers connected thereto, is primarily the level of radiation and their half-life period. Radium can be found at the top of the scale, whilst tritium is rather at the lower end. Radium has a half-life of 1600 years, for tritium, the half-life is 12.3 years. Creation and decay are also different, which will be dealt with later.

On the watch dial, we can find designations telling us something about the radioactive substances used, but this is not always the case, especially on earlier watches.

Some examples: Watch dials marked, 'Ra Swiss (Made) Ra' would indicate radium, 'T Swiss (Made) T' would indicate tritium emitting radioactivity of less than 7.5 millicuries. 'Swiss-T <25', would be tritium with radioactivity of up to 25 millicuries. Occasionally, but very rarely, also promethium was used and denoted with a 'P' or 'Pm'.

Just 'Swiss' could mean two things: Radium on dial and hands (if lumed in the earlier periods) or simply a watch made in Switzerland on later models, already lumed with Super-LumiNova or not lumed at all.

'L Swiss (Made) L' would point to LumiNova, the harmless and not radioactive material on later watches. Because of the almost exclusive use of LumiNova or Super-LumiNova nowadays, we do not find any such indications anymore on newly produced watches.

Radium (radium 226), half-life period: 1600 years.

The activation of the luminous paint was at first caused by radium (radium 226), especially on military watches and instruments. Radium, an alpha-emitter in the decay process, is a danger to health, to a lesser extent to the wearer of the watch, but to people involved in the production (especially in the application of the paint) or dealing with service and repairs.

The radium itself has some luminescent properties glowing blue. But that alone is too weak and not bright enough, and the amount needed to make it useful in this respect would require too much of it and its radiation would even be more harmful.

Over the years, the dangerous and unhealthy aspects of radium became widely known and it was gradually reduced until the early 1960s to a fraction of the applications starting in the early 1900s. In the year 1968, the use of radium on watches was banned, not hindering some collectors or even professionals in watch service and -repair shops to carelessly deal with the matter. The same applies to tritium.

The long half-life period of 1.600 years does not mean a glowing effect for centuries to come. The aging process of the luminous paint puts an end to everything a lot sooner, that's why vintage watches from the applicable period have long lost their luminous effects – a big danger, as many people believe that the radium has also gone.

Tritium, half-life period: 12.3 years.

By the end of the 1950s, up to the 1990s, weak radioactive isotopes like tritium or promethium became available and have subsequently replaced the more dangerous radium. It has the lowest radiotoxicity of all isotopes.

Tritium (^{3}H or T) is besides protium (^{1}H) and deuterium (^{2}H) a natural isotope of hydrogen (H, 1). Protium and deuterium are stable; tritium is unstable, which is the reason why it is radioactive. It emits electrons along with its beta-decay, which interact with the phosphorous material. Under exposure to beta-radiation, the luminous material is emitting protons in a typical color. The effect is fading much sooner compared to radium-lumed watches (half-life period of 1,600 years), with the light source becoming too dim with a useful end after 25 to 30 years.

In any case, this always goes along with the additional degradation of the luminous stuff, reducing the brightness and the overall effectiveness also for this reason.

As already mentioned, tritium is an expensive material (often more expensive than the rest of a cheaper type watch), and as producers were using as little as possible, we can often see a useful period of only 10 to 20 years.

The radiation is almost entirely absorbed by the luminous paint itself or shielded off by the watch case and watch crystal (if made from glass and not acrylic). To bond the tritium-gas as much as possible with the zinc sulfide, all is mixed with a special substance.

As Tritium is a volatile substance (when not bound), it can, as a whole and under certain conditions (bad sealing), penetrate to the outside. Tritium is not very radiotoxic but can get into the body and react there. The dangers have always been seen as negligible, until a study of a group of French-Belgian scientists came out in the year 2008, stating that the radiotoxic effects of tritium have so far been underestimated. It can deviate into the human DNA (genetic substance), which can be especially problematic. Separate from this, its beta radiation will not be effectively stopped by acrylic glass, especially when corroded through aging.

Theoretically, it would be possible to use any other beta-emitter, but tritium is well suited for this purpose. Some watch collectors like the yellowish, creamily patina on a vintage watch dial, caused by the tritium.

Tritium was used until a period when the first plastic watchcases came out. Unlike metal cases, tritium can penetrate through the plastic and be absorbed by the skin. A study of the University of Innsbruck, Austria, found a 10-times higher concentration in the urine of 108 test persons wearing tritium-lumed watches in plastic cases, than what has been measured within a comparison group. The test watches came from well know names on the dial, down to the usual garbage from Far East. Some producers had, already since 1992, replaced the dangerous tritium on plastic watches with harmless thermo-phosphates, activated through body heat.

Cheap plastic watches + tritium should seek proper disposal, instead of finding a way into collections. Even if the radioactive exposure is comparatively low, compared to the natural radiation, it's totally useless to wear such a watch.

As already mentioned, tritium, as an activator, is lately safely used in closed glass tubes (GTLS).

Hygienic measures

Radium is not part of the production of luminous paint anymore. When working with tritium, it has to be treated as an open radiation source, despite much lower radiation-hygienic parameters applicable to all the other isotopes used until then.

Proper protective measures, organization of the working process to avoid contamination of persons and objects, controls of people when leaving the workplace with UV light, and decontamination – if necessary – are a must.

Furthermore, material intended for cleaning hands, objects, work places, can only be used once and must be properly disposed of.

Hands, equipment, and objects exposed to contamination must be kept away from the mouth and the breathing zone.

Food, drinks, cosmetic articles are not allowed within the working area. The place must have sufficient ventilation, naturally or artificially.

The employees have to be regularly tested by measurement of the tritium content in the urine.

All of that is of course a strictly followed minimum standard in the community of vintage watch collectors and tinkerers – or is it not?

Well, it's all a matter of frequency and intensity, but it is certainly not a playground for careless activities.

ATOMS, MOLECULES AND OTHER PARTICLES

As we are frequently confronted with a variety of specific terms throughout the book, a few explanations:

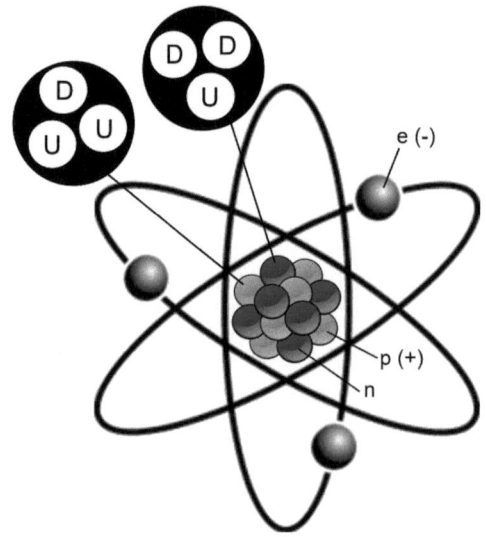

Atomic model: p = proton, n = neutron, e = electron.
U = Up-Quark and D = Down-Quark, they are parts
of protons (2 x U, 1 x D) and neutrons (2 x D, 1 x U)

Atoms are the smallest building blocks of matter, but not the smallest parts. They are composed of a **core (nucleus)** which contains **protons** and **neutrons** and **a hull** in or around which the **electrons** are circling the core.

The hull: There are several depictions around. The electrons are shown outside, on the edge, or within the hull. What concerns their path, there are also different views; some see them following a fixed orbit, some let them live in 'mathematically defined lounge areas' or 'probability densities' etc. The hull is supposed to have a diameter between 10.000- to 150.000 times larger than the core, whilst the comparably tiny core has 99.9% of the total mass.

Elements: As an example, a gold bar consists of billions of atoms of the same kind. The same goes for silver or any other element. Naturally, there must be a property of an atom, defining which ones come together as gold, and which ones as silver (or whatever). This property is the number of protons it has, identical with the atomic number (proton number) in the periodical chart of elements. Gold (au, 79) has 79 protons and silver (ag, 47) has 47 protons. So, your silver watchcase is almost gold, except for 32 protons missing in each of the atoms.

Neutral atoms have a neutral charge (they are electrically neutral) if they have the same number of **protons (+ charge)** and **electrons (- charge)**. **Neutrons** have no charge. If there is a surplus on either side, we speak of **ions** = atoms with an electrical charge. Positive charge overall = **cations**, negative charge overall = **anions**. **Molecules** (a combination of atoms) can also be called ions, if they have an electrical charge (+ or - overall). **Ionization** is the process by which an atom or molecule gets a positive charge by losing electrons. **Ionizing radiation** is particle- or electromagnetic radiation (alpha, beta, gamma, x-ray) with such a power, that it can remove electrons from atoms or molecules, converting them to ions (the atoms or molecules are **'ionized'**). In strict terms, ionization refers to the formation of a positive ion, but the name can also refer to the formation of a negative ion.

Protons, short definition: A proton (ancient Greek 'proto' = first) is an electrically charged (+) particle. The number of protons defines the chemical element.

Neutrons, short definition: A neutron (from the Latin word 'neutra/neutrum' – none of both, referring to the not existing positive- or negative charge) is a particle without any electrical charge. They are normally in the core together with the protons but can also be outside (free neutrons).

Electrons, short definition: Electrons (driving from the English word 'electron' and etymological from 'electric') are electrically charged (-) particles. They can be found circling in/around the hull of the atomic core.

Atoms, short definition: They consist of a core with protons (+ charge) and neutrons (no charge), and a hull with electrons (- charge). The number of protons defines the chemical element. The protons (U+U+D) and neutrons (D+D+U) consist of Up-Quarks (U) and Down-Quarks (D).

Mass number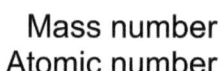
Atomic number

In the above example for the isotope radium 226 (chemical symbol 'Ra'), the top (mass-) number defines the quantity of protons and neutrons combined (here 226), the bottom (atomic number) the quantity of protons (here 88). The difference would then be the quantity of neutrons (result here 138).

If an atomic core is called nuclide, it is unambiguously defined by its mass number and atomic number. Atomic cores of the same element with the same quantity of protons, but with a different quantity of neutrons, are called isotopes, which are thus a special form of nuclides.

But wait, there is more!

Anti-particles: positron for the electron, anti-neutron for the neutron, anti-proton for the proton. They are of the same mass, but with the opposite electrical charge.

The **positron (anti-electron)**, for instance, is the anti-particle (or the anti-matter-counterpart) of the electron. It can, as one variant, be produced by radioactive decay (positron emission). It is identical to an electron, has the same mass, but the opposite electrical charge (+). When positron and electron collide, they destroy each other (annihilation), producing **photons** (which are then both, particle and anti-particle combined). Positrons produced in natural radioactive decay quickly annihilate themselves with electrons and produce gamma rays.

Lately, new discoveries have broken down protons and neutrons even further, as smaller particles have been found, called 'Quarks' (**Up-Quark** and **Down Quark**). A proton consists of two Up-Quarks and one Down-Quark. The neutron consists of two Down-Quarks and one Up-Quark.

Still not the end: There had been recent findings, that even the electrons, so far considered to be undividable and about 2000 times smaller in mass than the protons or neutrons, consist themselves of smaller particles, so-called **quasiparticles: orbiton** and **spinon**.

Then we still have the **neutrinos** and **anti-neutrinos**. A neutrino is electrically neutral and does normally not react with matter but has a part in the beta -minus decay. Not all is known about those neutrinos, except that their mass is very small or even equal to zero. Nevertheless, there are supposedly many of them around, coming through space, from the sun, the soil, nuclear reactors, or accelerator experiments. As neutrinos do not react with matter, they can penetrate through massive shielding, e.g. through the entire Mother Earth.

Neutrino and anti-neutrino differ by their helicity. Spin and flying direction left = neutrino, spin and flying direction right = anti-neutrino.

And then, we also have the **anti-matter** (anti-particles). We know that 'something' exists, but what about the existence of 'nothing'? Does nothing (or the opposite of matter) not exist? On the contrary – it does! It would be too far leading to deal with that phenomenon in more detail, therefore just so much:

If you own a specific watch, it is also a fact, that someone else doesn't own it. The ownership is a fact like the non-ownership is a fact. If you miss a deal on the Internet platform, you represent the anti-matter to the matter of ownership by someone else – leaving aside that you could have the better position on some deals that have proven to be not so good afterward.

As we all know already and only for the sake of completeness:

A combination of several atoms makes a **molecule**, like H_2O, the water molecule, 2 x H = hydrogen, 1 x O = oxygen. It is therefore composed of two atoms of hydrogen and one atom of oxygen.

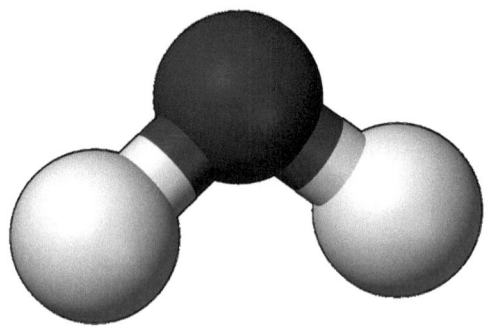

In the case of radium 226 on watch dials as an activator of the luminous material, we are dealing with an isotope within the decay chain from Uranium 238 to lead 206 (see separate chapter). Radium 226 has a half-life period of 1600 years. It is basically, in its pure form, an alpha-emitter, but further down the chain, we also find beta-radiation. There is also gamma-radiation as a secondary product of alpha- and beta decay.

In the case of tritium (T or 3H) with the same function as radium in view of activating a luminous substance, we are looking at a natural isotope of hydrogen (H, 1). Its atomic core consists of one proton and two neutrons. It decays in one step with a half-life period of 12.3 years, under emission of an electron and an anti-neutrino, into the stable helium isotope 3He (one of the two stable Helium isotopes besides 4He).

DECAY CHAIN OF TRITIUM

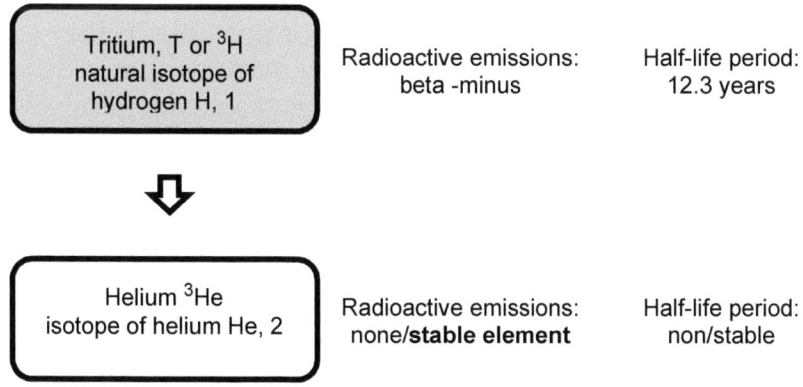

The long decay chain with radium 226 in the line, is shown later in the book.

33

RADIOACTIVITY, RADIOACTIVE DECAY, TYPES OF RADIATION, EFFECTS ON HEALTH

Radioactivity is the spontaneous occurrence of decay, down the decay chain, and emitting alpha-, beta, and gamma radiations within a random but overall stable process.

There are many critical questions about the randomness of the decay. How can that all be totally random without any kind of systematology, especially as we define specific half-life periods for each element? The scientists are seeking explanations in statistics, perhaps like the 70% of all perpetrators become recidivists after they have served their sentence – you just don't know which ones.

The Radioactive Decay Law (Rutherford-Soddy) even makes this a firm rule. All random, merely a matter of chance, only the order cannot be told. But all goes on at a very precise rate overall.

Nuclides or isotopes (same or similar thing, depending on the use of these terms), can be stable or unstable. If they are unstable, they are seeking stability by decay within a decay chain until a stable state at a final level is reached. This always goes along with emitting radioactive radiation.

The activity of a radioactive substance is defined by the number of atom cores decaying within a second. The physical unit is called Becquerel (Bq).

What concerns the radiations in the context of this book, we distinguish between three different fundamental types: **alpha (α)-, beta (β)- and gamma (γ) radiation**. The radiations of the decaying elements can be more or less penetrating, also over large distances. The main danger, however, when speaking of lumed vintage watches, occurs mainly if substances are inhaled or ingested into the body.

All have in common, that this effect comes from very tiny and fast-moving particles. Because of their high amount of energy, they can break up chemical bonds and cause severe damage to living and dead material.

Further dangers exist in form of possible damage of the DNA (genetic substance) only discernible in the progeny.

Alpha radiation

Alpha (α)-emitters are radioactive substances, which decay into an alpha particle and a positively charged remaining core.

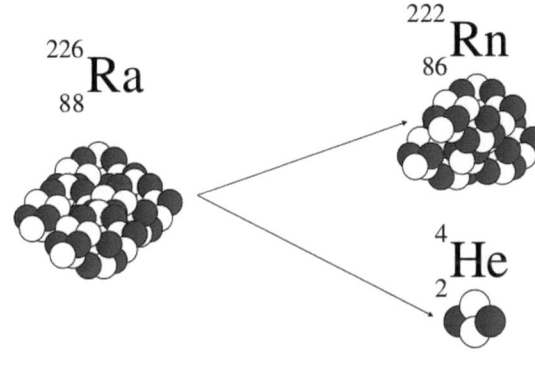

The particles emitted during an alpha decay correspond to the core of helium atoms, which are 2 protons and 2 neutrons with a double positive charge. The mass number (protons and neutrons combined) is therefore reduced by 4, the atomic number (protons only) by 2. The excess electrons are transferred to other atoms.

Radium 226, one of the substances acting as an activator of the zinc sulfide contained in the luminous paint, has a mass number of 226 and an atomic number of 88. With 2 protons and 2 neutrons gone, the next decay product in the line is Radon 222, with a mass number of 222 (4 less in total) and an atomic number of 86 (2 protons less).

Alpha-radiation has a lot of energy, but only a short reach and can be easily stopped. In water, the energy is lost already after a few micrometers (1 micrometer =0.001 millimeters). In open air, already a sheet of paper is sufficient to shield off alpha-radiation.

How can alpha-radiation affect the human body?

It can hardly penetrate the skin from the outside. However, it becomes highly dangerous if it is digested or inhaled. Once in the body, it can have a direct effect on the human tissue, whereby it can concentrate the unhealthy, in the end perhaps deadly effects, on a small space. This becomes a big problem if it is not excreted from the body. The substance can be deposited in the body and have a lot more time to create substantial damage. For smokers, it can be that 'little extra' that adds to the probability of lung cancer.

Alpha radiation can also be found in cigarette smoke. The naturally occurring radioactive polonium 210 settles at the little hairs of the tobacco leaves and is inhaled into the lung when smoking. Because of the short reach of the alpha radiation, the total energy is absorbed by the body. In the bronchial tubes of smokers, one does usually find three or four times more of the normal amount of this substance.

Nevertheless, this type of radiation is also used in the medical sector in a positive way. The alpha-radiation can destroy tumor cells, whereby the surrounding tissue is only marginally affected because of the very short reach.

Beta radiation

Beta-decay (β) is a radioactive reaction with a beta ray of a fast-energetic electron **or** positron and a neutrino emitted from the atomic core.

A neutron transforms into a proton by change of the Up- and Down-Quarks within (from D+D+U to U+U+D) and an electron (+ neutrino) is emitted (electron emission).

Vice versa, a proton transforms into a neutron by change of the Up- and Down-Quarks within (from U+U+D to D+D+U), and a positron (+ neutrino) is emitted (positron emission).

In both cases, the type of the core (nucleus) is changed. Neither the emitted particle nor its associated neutrino did exist prior to the decay process. The atom is seeking a more stable state, which goes on until a totally stable stage is reached.

The **two types of beta decay** are called beta-minus- and beta-plus decay: **Beta-minus (β-)** = conversion of a neutron into a proton, creating an electron and an electron anti-neutrino, which are leaving the core. **Beta-plus (β+)** = conversion of a proton into a neutron, creating a positron and an electron neutrino.

We could also look at the difference between hard- and weak beta-radiation, but that would be too far leading, especially as the border lines are not so clearly defined.

Unlike alpha radiation, the beta radiation does penetrate through the watch crystal (especially the acrylic type).

How does it affect the human body?

Especially insidious: beta radiation can have delayed health effects. *Any* amount of exposure may lead to cancer or reproductive cell damage. Since the effects are not immediately visible, there is no way to determine beforehand any reverse effects, which can arise months to years afterward. A large dose can however result in sickness already after a short timespan.

Besides inhalation or ingestion, also direct outside exposure is extremely hazardous, especially during pregnancy. Such a direct exposure can cause burns of the skin, loss of hair, or overall weakness. Further effects: nervous system damage or weakening of the immune system. Beta particles, like alpha particles, can be also used in the medical field for diagnosis, treatment, and imaging. Beta radiation is a fast process that penetrates human skin. It can break chemical bonds and destroy human cells.

Gamma-radiation

Gamma-radiation (γ-radiation) – energy-rich radioactive waves with an ultra-short wavelength – is the most penetrating and most far-reaching. It comes along with alpha- and beta radiation (alpha- and beta decay).

Contrary to the other radiations, it does not consist of charged particles like alpha and beta but is electromagnetic radiation/photon radiation (same as radio waves, light, UV-radiation, or X-ray).

It is far-reaching and can easily penetrate the human body. It can only be shielded off by meter-thick concrete walls or thick layers of lead. In this connection, we find the term and measuring standard 'half-value depth', after which the radiation is reduced to half its intensity in a specific material.

Gamma radiation is identical with X-radiation, apart from its origination (gamma in the core, X-ray in the hull), and is in a different but overlapping wave spectrum. It is the most energetic known form of electromagnetic radiation

Gamma-radiation can only occur upon the decay of an atomic core or as a **secondary product of an alpha- and beta decay**. In nature, they can be the result of a decay of radioactive substances or cosmic radiation from the sky.

How does it affect the human body?

Through penetration, easily and intensively into and through the human body, it leaves a trail of damage on its way, especially when coming along in high dosage.

In general, only the tissue is affected that has been exposed to the radiation. The destructive effect exists initially only for the time the human body is exposed to such a source, but damage can also occur with some delay.

If we look at the type of radiation, the intensity (energy), the type of tissue affected, and the thickness of the material affected: The ability to penetrate is the smallest for the alpha radiation and the largest for the gamma radiation. What concerns the absorption capacity, the ratios are exactly the other way around. The effect of the radiation is often only noticed in connection with the regeneration process of the human cells.

In the medical area, gamma-radiation is used in cancer therapy and -diagnostic in form of the radioactive element cobalt (cobalt isotope ^{60}Co). It can also be used to preserve food. In an apple, for instance, it can kill pathogens or vermin: also maturing- or rotting processes can be influenced, but these are highly disputed procedures.

Type of radiation	Relative size of particles	Amount of energy	Relative penetrating ability
Alpha	large	much	Poor - will not penetrate human skin
Beta	small	little	Medium - can penetrate human skin
Gamma	very small	little	Good - can easily pass through the human body

Radioactive emission and radioactive dust can destroy acrylic watch crystals over time. They cause fine cracks, which makes some parts look like 'frozen'.

The markers on this dial had originally been lumed, but the luminous paint has fallen off, almost completely. This, of course, means, that the particles must be all around on the dial, mostly versus the edges, and will inevitably fall out when the watch is opened. It bears the danger that they are inhaled or picked up with the fingers. The fine particles of crumbled luminous paint can be made visible under UV light.

X-radiation, X-ray: To complete the picture, it should also be mentioned, that we are – to some very minor extend – also confronted with X-Radiation in the decay process of the activators of the luminous paint. It is basically of the same type as gamma radiation, in different, but overlapping wave spectrum and can also be distinguished by its origination. X-radiation occurs with the change of velocity of charged particles when beta-radiation penetrates a material.

The lottery: Those, who deal with radioactivity, also have the chance to participate in an uncontrollable gamble.

The deleterious effect of ionizing radiation on human tissue can be divided into two types: **deterministic (non-stochastic)** and **stochastic** (the 'lottery'). **Deterministic radiation damage (cell death)** only occurs once a threshold of exposure is exceeded. The severity increases, as the dose increases, from harmless to deadly.

Stochastic radiation damage (cell change) is all different. Any amount of radiation can be harmful. There is no threshold dose below which no damage occurs. The individual dose does not determine the severity, but only its probability of occurrence. Stochastic effects take place during regular cell division. The cells keep their ability to divide, but the DNA is changed and passed on to the next generations (genetic defects).

Madame Curie, two times Noble Price winner in her lab (1921). She has coined the term 'radioactive' and, together with her husband, she has discovered the elements polonium and radium.

Remnants of the radium mixing apparatus of the US Radium Corp. from the early times when radium was applied on watch dials and hands (see also the last chapter 'Radium Girls').

DECAY CHAIN - URANIUM 238 to LEAD 206
Emissions: alpha = α, beta = β, gamma = γ

Element		Emissions	Half-life
238 Uranium isotope of U. 92		α, γ	4,5 billion years
⬇			
234 Thorium isotope of Th, 90		β, γ	24 days
⬇			
234 Protactinium isotope of Pa, 91		β, γ	6.7 hours (234 Pa) 1.2 minutes (234m Pa)
⬇			
234 Uranium isotope of U. 92		α, γ	245.000 years
⬇			
230 Thorium isotope of Th, 90		α, γ	75.000 years
⬇			
Radium 226 isotope of Ra, 88		α, γ	1.600 years
⬇			
222 Radon isotope of Rn, 86		α	3.8 days
⬇ …	to be continued on the next page		

… continued from the previous page

Element	Element	Emissions	Half-Life
218 Polonium isotope of Po, 84	⤵	99.98%, α 0.02%, β	3.1 minutes 3.1 minutes
99,98% ⬇	0,02% ⬇		
214 Lead isotope Pb, 82	218 Astatine isotope At, 85	lead = β,γ astatine = α	26.8 minutes 1.5 seconds
⬇	⤴		
214 Bismuth isotope of Bi, 83	⤵	99.98%, β, γ 0.02%, α	19.9 minutes 19,9 minutes
99,98% ⬇	0,02% ⬇		
214 Polonium isotope of Po, 84	210 Thallium isotope of Tl, 81	Polonium = α Thallium = β	0,00016 seconds 1.3 minutes
⬇	⤴		
210 Lead isotope of Pb, 82		β, γ	22.3 years
⬇			
210 Bismuth isotope of Bi, 83	⤵	99.99987% β 0.00013% α	5 days 5 days
99.99987% ⬇	0.00013% ⬇		
210 Polonium isotope of Po, 84	206 Thallium isotope of Tl, 81	Polonium = α, γ Thallium = β	138 days 4 minutes
⬇	⤴		
206 Lead / stable isotope of Pb, 82		**none / stable**	**stable element**

To make it very simple (after all, we are just watch collectors): The way of the uranium 238 to lead 206 is like dripping from bucket to bucket with different size holes in the bottom, whilst at the same changing to another element *It's an ongoing procedure, which starts immediately on all levels.* The half-life period defines the time it needs to lose half of the volume in each bucket and again half of what is left. Therefore, we must have more than radium on dial and hands, although only 2.5% of the Radium 226 went into the next stage (and further) after 80 years (50% in 1600 years). Mathematically, this would never end, but we can't create fractions of an atom. Each individual bucket should be completely empty after 10 half-life periods.

STRONTIUM 90 – THE BONE SEEKER

Strontium 90 as an activator of the luminous substances on watch dials and hands has only been rarely used, so chances that a collector becomes unknowingly 'the lucky winner' of such a timepiece at the Internet auction are not very high, but these watches are still around.

It is highly difficult (impossible for the normal collector) to determine its existence in the large pile of lumed vintage watches floating around in collections or on the market.

Its short half-life period of 28.8 years might give some comfort, but you should remember, that only half of that is gone at the end of this period, then another half of what is left, and so on. The next element in the decay chain, the isotope yttrium 90, has only a half-life period of 64 hours before everything has fallen down into a safe bucket of zirconium 90, a stable and non-radioactive isotope.

The latter was not stated to provide arguments for the disciples of the 'it's-all-not-so-bad' theories. On the contrary, because of the high dangers to human health connected with this element, it is necessary to give the matter a little more scope.

The time strontium 90 can remain in the body (biological half-life period) can vary from 2 weeks up to some decades, possibly 50 years, which is due to the complex mutation within the body.

Detecting radioactive radiation (and its type) is relatively easy. It is, however, something totally different if one wants to determine the different elements and everything existent down the decay chain. Simply impossible for a watch collector with amateur equipment and difficult enough for professional labs.

Strontium 90 is really something special and not called 'bone seeker' for nothing. The main problem is that it has a biochemical behavior similar to calcium, an element essential to the human body (bones, teeth).

When the stuff is reaching the inside of the body (by ingestion with contaminated food or water), a lot of the dose gets excreted, but then, all remaining strontium 90 is deposited in the bones and the bone marrow, with minor portions reaching the blood and soft tissues, which can cause bone cancer, cancer of adjacent tissues and leukemia. A direct relationship between the amount of strontium 90 deposited and the occurrence of cancer has been proven.

It is all around us in significant amounts, as a product of nuclear fission, originating from nuclear reactors, especially (but not only) after an accident, and comes along as fallout from nuclear tests. It can be found in larger doses in the teeth of people born after 1963, as a consequence of the atomic bomb tests. Strontium 90 was, together with the isotopes of cesium (134 cesium) and iodine (iodine 131), amongst the most important harmful isotopes affecting human health after the Chernobyl disaster.

Promethium 147

Just briefly mentioned - the isotope promethium 147 (rarely used as an activator for the luminous paint). It has a beta-minus decay with a half-life period of 2.64 years into samarium 147, but the radioactive samarium 147 (alpha decay) will then be around for a while, because of its half-life period of 106 billion years. The final stage is the stable isotope neodymium 143. As the decay starts immediately, also the samarium 147 will come along right from the start.

So much for: 'the radioactive stuff on my watch must be gone, I don't see any glowing anymore'.

Another isotope of Samarium (153) is used in nuclear medicine (by injection into the blood) to destroy diseased tissue, with only minor effects on the surrounding healthy tissue. It also has a therapeutic use in the treatment of thyroid diseases, painful bone metastases, or rheumatic joint pain.

DECAY CHAIN OF STRONTIUM 90

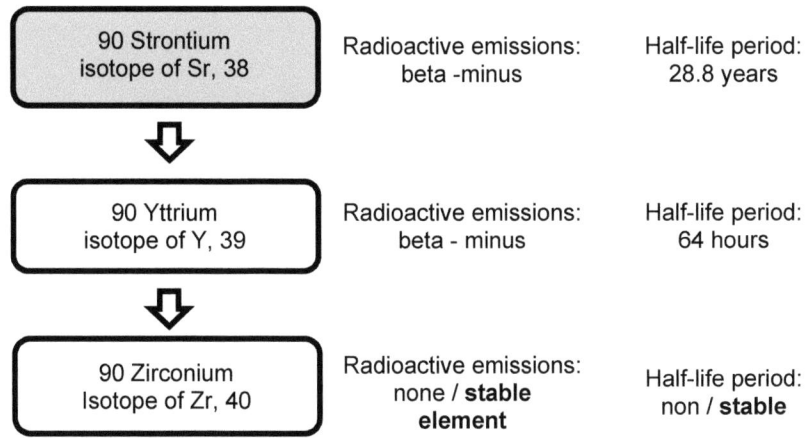

DECAY CHAIN OF PROMETHIUM 147

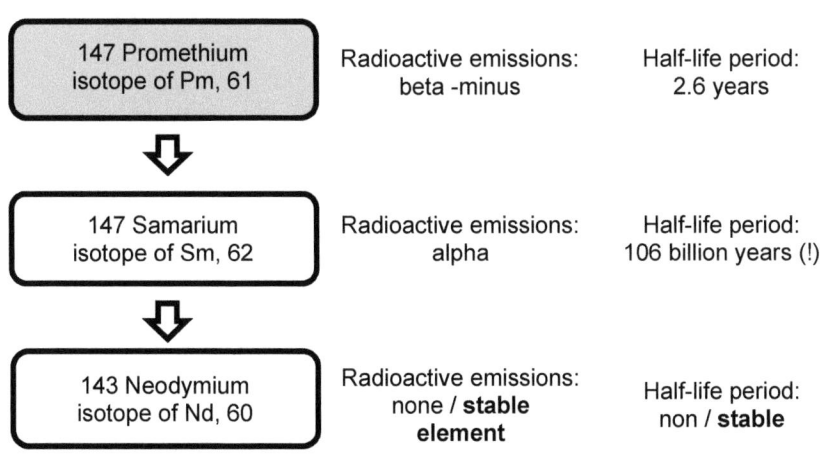

47

MEASURING RADIOACTIVE RADIATION

For the purpose of this book, no reference is made relating to any threshold values of radiation in view of dangers to human health at whatever level. This depends on too many factors – distance, time, duration of exposure, long-term effects, etc. And, last, but not least, no personal opinions have been expressed within a sphere of discussion, where even the experts often largely disagree.

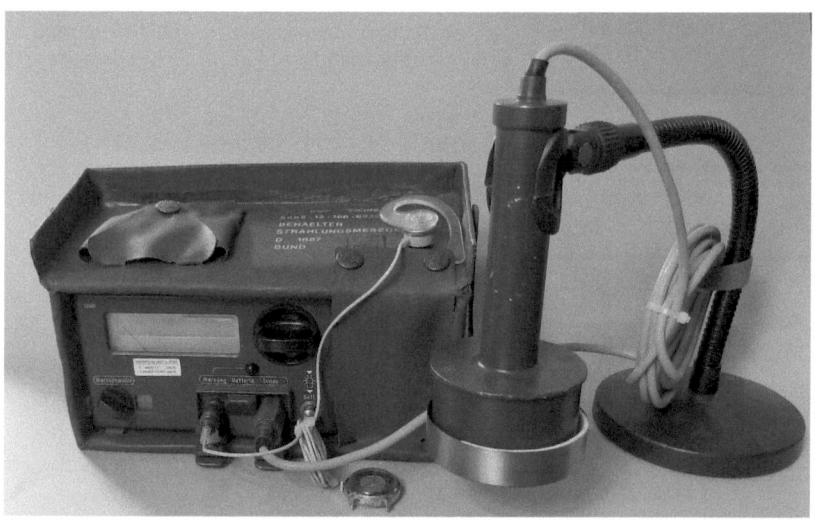

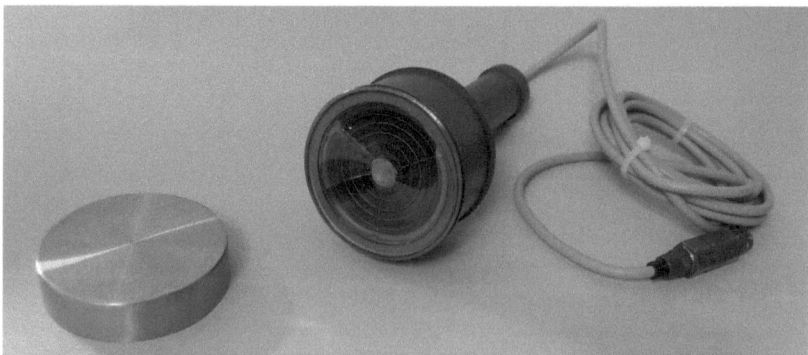

Above: SV-500 Frieseke & Hoepfner/FAG Kugelfischer with big probe

Before you put any money into any equipment measuring radioactive radiation, you should be aware of a few things.

There is a large number of such devices on the market, ranging from professional and reliable, down to cheap or even dubious quality. If the instrument does not have the necessary quality (check tests, feedback, etc.), forget about it. You should also not fall into the trap of buying a thing intended for other use, often based on unclear descriptions. EMF (Electromagnetic Field) measuring devices detect electromagnetic radiation from electromagnetic fields ('electro smog') coming from microwave ovens, cell phones, computers, hi-fi equipment, power lines, wireless networks, radio waves, baby phones, energy-saving bulbs, heatable waterbeds, and lots more.

Gamma radiation, coming from lumed watches containing radium- or tritium, as a reaction to alpha- and beta decay, is electromagnetic radiation as well, but in a totally different area of the spectrum. It can therefore not be measured with normal EMF devices. Its dramatically shorter wavelength is far out of the range (see below).

	Wave length	Frequency	Units of 1 Hertz (full swings per second)
Microwave	12.22cm	2. 455 GHz	2,455,000,000,000
Gamma radiation	10 picometer	30 EHz	30,000,000,000,000,000,000,000

These EMF devices still leave the Internet platforms every day as 'Geiger-counters', and some friends of 'richly lumed' vintage watches wonder why they can't detect any radiation coming from the dial, not even gamma. The right device (for detecting radioactive radiation on dial and hands) should pick up alpha- (α), beta- (β), and gamma (γ) radiation, preferably with a possibility to separate them. Some of these instruments can only pick up beta- and gamma radiation and are also not suitable for our use.

Besides the device itself, the right probe/detector makes a major difference, not only in view of what it can pick up, but also considering how reliable it works.

You might want to go for used equipment, often the better choice given a certain price. The question of calibration is not that important if it isn't far out. In the end, you only want to have a rough, but good estimate, as also many other factors play an important role.

The device shown at the beginning of the chapter has been acquired used but in a fairly new condition from army surplus. The large probe, picking up alpha-, beta- and gamma radiation, was purchased separately. If the instrument itself cannot separate the different types of radiations (most all in the affordable range can't do that), the separation of alpha-, beta- and gamma radiation is quite easy, following a simple procedure:

The measurements and calculations described on the next page are from the left watch shown below (results from the right watch are also shown in the table at the bottom):

Above left: 1950s Junghans. Extremely strong radiation, dial 'burned' brown, luminous paint crumbling, especially on the hands, with loose particles on the dial. The old crystal (heavily cracked) had already been replaced. Above right: Anker wristwatch from the 1950s (radium lumed). The original crystal is cracked, caused by the radioactive emissions.

Steps taken to separate alpha-, beta- and gamma radiation, measurements from the left watch on page 53 (you can also do it the other way around):

1. The (acrylic) watch crystal was removed, as it would otherwise shield off the alpha radiation. When removing the watch crystal, one should really know how to do this. That is the moment, even more dangerous than opening the case at the back, that the radioactive particles find their way out. The watch crystal can immediately crack under the pressure of the crystal lift, because it is often in bad shape due to the long exposure to radioactive substances, normally not a problem with old crystals of an unlumed watch. Here, the crystal had recently been changed. (The crystal on the right watch on the previous page cracked under pressure, as feared). **The reading was 100 mrad/h**.

2. The crystal was put back on, leaving out alpha radiation. The reading for beta and gamma combined was 17 mrad/h. **The alpha radiation is therefore 83 mrad/h**.

3. An aluminum cap was put on the probe, shutting out alpha and gamma radiation. The reading was **4 mrad/h for the remaining gamma radiation**. Alpha and beta combined are therefore 96 mrad/h. As we already had determined the value for alpha with 83mrad/h, the value for **beta = 13 mrad/h**. This aluminum cap is also a practical and effective protection for the delicate probe.

Measurements (close distance) mrad/h:	α + β + γ	β + γ	γ	Breakdown mrad/h:
Junghans watch (left/page 53)	100	17	4	α = 83, β = 13, γ = 4
Anker watch (right/page 53)	4	1.5	0.5	α = 2.5, β = 1.0, γ = 0.5

The radioactivity of a substance is measured in the number of nuclei, which decay per specific unit of time.

Activity: Becquerel (Bq), old unit Curie (Ci), 1 Ci = 37 billion Becquerel.

Energy dose: Gray (Gy), old unit Rad (rd), 1 Gray = 100 rad.

Energy dose rate: Gray per second ($Gy\ s^{-1}$), old unit Rad per second ($rd\ s^{-1}$), 1 ($Gy\ s^{-1}$) = 100 ($rd\ s^{-1}$)

Equivalent dose: Sievert (Sv), old unit Rem (rem), 1 Sievert = 100 Rem

Equivalent dose rate: Sievert per second ($Sv\ s^{-1}$), old unit Rem per second ($rem\ s^{-1}$), 1 ($Sv\ s^{-1}$) = 100 ($rem\ s^{-1}$)

Radiography, x-ray therapeutics and radium therapy (1915)

PURCHASE OF LUMED VINTAGE WATCHES

In many cases, you will not be able to determine the substances of the lumed paint, unless marked on the dial. You must simply make your own judgment according to the time period, but you will never be able to distinguish between radium and strontium or other substances, and activities are everywhere along the decay chain.

So, be careful when acquiring lumed vintage watches (radium, strontium, and even tritium type). Leave the case closed if you are not absolutely sure what you are doing. Already the 'movement shot' – the opening of the bottom just for an image of the movement – should be done with the utmost care, not to speak of working on the watch.

Some watches are 'front loaders', which means that they have to be opened at the front by removing the crystal. As the radioactively contaminated stuff is everywhere after the luminous paint has started to crumble, it can fall out and do its harm.

Remember: the main dangers do not primarily come from the radioactive radiation reaching the body from the outside, but the substances 'go to work' once they got inside the body and that can be a long process without any intermediate warnings.

Run-of-the mill products (and not collectible timepieces or interesting models), combined with beat-up cases, destroyed crystals, luminous paint crumbling and falling out of the hands and from the numbers and markers, should lead to the conclusion: *Everything has its time,* and some of those things had their time long ago. Whatever, they could still serve a good purpose as demonstration items in connection with measuring radioactive radiation, if handled carefully and correctly.

RADON ISSUES

The next in line down the uranium 238 to lead 206 decay chain, after radium 226, is radon 222, which poses a special threat. Here, we do not talk about radioactive particles on dials and hands, which can be inhaled or digested, but about a radioactive gas.

Vintage watch collectors have a new enemy: radon

- The invisible killer that's bigger than carbon monoxide
- Avoid poisoning your family with radon
- No amount of radon is truly safe
- Radon has a place near the top of the list of concerns
- Radon, a prime cancer-causing agent

In recent times, the danger arising from radon gas comes more and more into the focus of environmental discussions, having triggered worldwide activities and warnings, including governmental recommendations and regimentation, although its nothing new to science, where the negative health effects had already been observed in the 16th century, without much knowledge about (lung-) cancer and the exact cause.

At first, it must be mentioned that this mainly refers to radon gas emitted from the natural environment, when uranium in soil and rocks breaks down. Radon 222 is the next in line within the uranium decay chain after radium 226, as shown in the chart on the pages 42/43.

It can creep into enclosed spaces, like homes and offices, thereby posing a threat to inhabitants or people working there. If diluted outside, it is of no concern. Vice versa, exposure to high levels of radon gas in indoor air is the second largest cause of lung cancer after smoking.

Along with governmental guidelines and regulations, safe levels and upper limits of radon gas have been determined worldwide, with different values depending on the country. A generally accepted action level, as published by the WHO – World Health Organization, is 100 Bq/m³ or 2.7 pCi/L, depending on the measurand used (conversion factor approx. 1 pCi/L = 37 Bq/m³). The unit pCi/L refers to picocuries (curies / and old measurement) per liter, the unit Bq/m³ (becquerel the new standard unit) per m³. One becquerel is defined as the quantity of radioactive material in which one nucleus decays per second. In the European Community, the danger level has been set at 300 Bq/m³, which cannot surprise, when danger levels of all sorts are usually elevated and phase-out periods prolonged, following the usual lobbying activities or the tactic of postponement.

There are several different radon-isotopes, but radon 222 is the one of greatest concerns. Because of its half-life period of 3.8 days, it can accumulate in building environments. The other two radon-isotopes have much shorter half-life periods, radon 220 ('thoron', 55.6 seconds) and radon 219 ('actinion', 3.7 seconds). They are, however, present somewhere else and not in the uranium 238 to lead 206 decay chain and have nothing to do with the luminous paint on the watch dials.

More and more reliable measuring devices are coming to the market at reasonable price levels for home use (as usual, with a lot of inferior or even useless instruments also floating around) or very expensive instruments for professional operators, but there is also the possibility of renting, which includes an external analysis afterward.

As there are oodles of documents available on this subject on the Net, also what concerns measurements to be taken and how, down to the influence on real estate prices, I will leave it at this what concerns the general aspects.

Now, what has all this to do with radium lumed vintage watches? Not very much, one would tend to say, but recently, also such watches appeared on the radon-danger scene.

In the year 2018, the UNESCO has supported worldwide studies dealing with the dangers coming from radon gas in closed environments, with universities around the globe participating.

As most of the studies concentrated on natural radon gas and the dangers in closed environments, two universities in Great Britain, the Kingston University and the University of Northampton have looked at another source of danger: watches – especially military watches – with radium lumed dials and hands, also emitting radon gas.

Other sources, besides glow-in-the-dark watches and clocks, or collected airplane instruments with radioluminescent paint, would be photo lenses (coating) from a certain period, ceramics made until the 1970s, canary glass, cloisonné jewelry, compasses, granite plates in the kitchen and around the house or certain concrete products.

The findings, based on 30 Second World-era military watches, have been dramatic. The entire collection gave rise to a hazardous radon concentration of approx. 67 times the domestic (UK) action level of 200 BQ/m^3 and over 134 times higher than the domestic (UK) target level of 100 Bq/m^3. Three watches in particular even had substantially higher readings than the average, with one watch measured at 1,200 Bq/m^3. The report concludes, that these watches have the potential to pose a significant hazard to the collectors and their families, with smokers particularly at risk.

Also, the opening of such watches without appropriate precautions is not recommended in the study, due to the dangers arising from radium 226 (as described in the book). Furthermore, it had been recommended not to wear such watches – and if stored in a box, the lid should be lifted outside the house, to allow the built-up gas to rapidly dissipate.

If one would criticize this valuable scientific contribution, there are a few points which could be mentioned, especially as the study did not solely concentrate on those watches, but also made a few comments about other unnatural sources besides watches with radioluminescent paint, too hastily declaring them more or less harmless, e. g. based on a single vase with a special type of enamel measured. We could have had totally different results with 30 vases measured and only one watch in comparison.

Moreover, not all of such radon-emitting items have been mentioned, so it would have been better to just generally refer to other possible radium emitters in the house. Recommending to carry the collector's box into the open before lifting the lid (minimizing radon danger) and then, when it comes to radium hazards, just a meager and unspecific statement like 'appropriate measures' is not very helpful, when dealing with that issue.

A watchmaker in the research team would have been highly valuable, explaining different cases, sealings, etc. to complete the picture and to explain the various types of work on opened watches (dangers arising from radium), including the removal of hands, the dial, the crystal and the dangers of particles getting onto the workbench. Also, a larger and statistically more reliable number of watches, not limited to the WWII military type, could have been more meaningful.

What concerns radon hazards from radium lumed watches, all, of course, has to be seen in a combination of things in the house, the prevailing natural sources, the location in the building, the ventilation habits, and so forth.

I have conducted my own experiments, with the clear result, that those watches, even the less heavily lumed, are strong and constant radon gas emitters. We also know that this is an uninterrupted process for thousands of years. In order not to mix measured results with the constantly changing conditions in the air, I made my test on a smaller scale in an airtight glass container. I left it bottom down with a sealing on top, which is more effective, as radon gas is heavier than air. The measuring device used is highly sensitive and can show results already after 10 minutes, as opposed to others, which need a day or longer.

I have chosen four watches, all less harmful than any military watch in this respect. Two pocket watches, one of them was my grandfather's and another one, which was my first watch, where I am even not absolutely certain that it has radioluminescent radium paint. In addition, I took two wristwatches (as shown on page 53).

Note: This was just a rudimentary test. The measurements have not been extrapolated to higher air volumes, which would result in substantially lower values in the dispersion, and merely serve as a simple demonstration of 'activity'.

58

Left: 1950s and 1960s Kienzle pocket watches, 1950s Junghans and 1950s Anker wristwatch. Right: glass jar with RadonEye inside, a reliable, very fast and affordable radon measuring device, perfectly suitable for home use. Controlled by a Smartphone app, with readings also shown on the device itself.

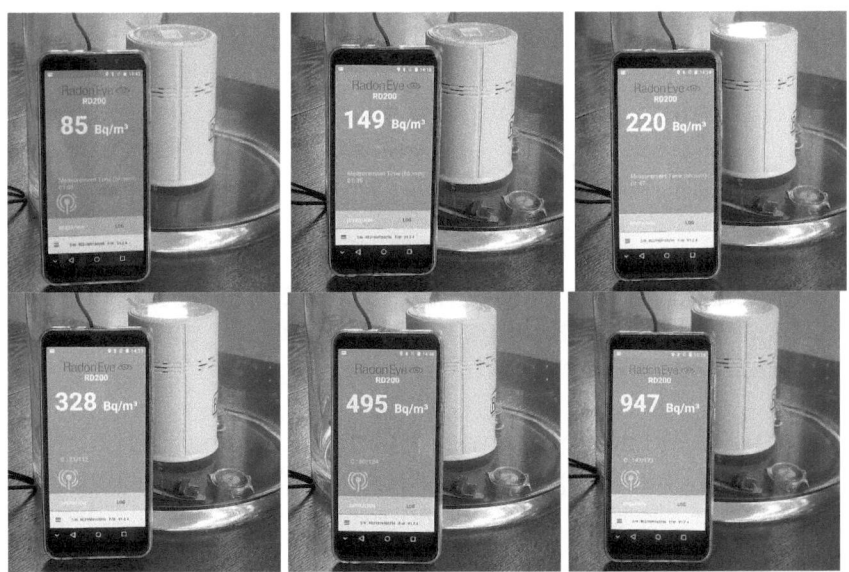

After a very short space of time, the radon concentration increased from 85 Bg/m³ (normal value measured in the room) to a dangerous level of 947 Bq/m³. I interrupted the test at this stage. The device is calibrated for a long time, but extreme measurements over a longer period might make an earlier calibration necessary. Of course, this all happened in a small and closed volume but clearly shows the enormous radioactivity.

REPLACING LUMINOUS PAINT ON WATCH DIALS AND HANDS

The replacement of radium- as well as tritium-activated luminous paint, is a big issue amongst watch collectors, sometimes even turning into an obsession.

Of course, a watch in its original condition is always a more collectible item, but common sense should also be part of the overall considerations. The question also comes along in connection with repairs and replacements of mechanical parts.

The slightest optical improvement of the dial is already (rightly) classified as 're-dial'. A sloppy job will make the watch close to worthless for some, but even a good restoration has its negative image in this respect.

'Authentic' is the magic phrase. Dirt or aging becomes patina, even water staining, and the no longer functioning of the lume makes it a rare watch – unchanged and original.

But wait! What do you mean with unchanged? Of course, something has changed – drastically changed: the ability to glow in the dark. Practically nothing of that left, whilst the dangers of radium and its decay products are still there. And it is even worse! The luminous paint has started to fall apart and its particles are lying everywhere, on and around the dial, and is, to some extent, not in a bound form anymore.

Does 'all original' make the watch worth a lot more, like a veteran vehicle with leaking tires and a broken clutch?

No, that all has to be kept original, even if you don't know if you had been the 'lucky winner' of a rare vintage watch of the 1950s with strontium 90 on the dial and hands.

And then, the worst that can happen in the life of a hardcore fan of originality: He gives the watch away for a service, and the well-meaning shop job replaces the hands or the luminous paint. It's already bad enough if some manufacturers are polishing cases or the buckle on the wristband or even dare to change an over-well-thumbed crown.

Some watchmakers (and even large companies) refuse to work on such watches, especially if they come from unknown sources (also in view of unknown radioactive substances used). Even if the timepieces came from their own production many moons ago (if the company should still be alive and in direct successorship) they often shy away from a service or repair.

But if they agree – or a friendly watchmaker – such a replacement of the old luminous paint would increase the *practical* value and simultaneously get rid of the dangers.

Some seem to forget, that professionals in some countries are obliged to follow strict legal provisions and must dispose of old and crumbly luminous paint containing radioactive substances, once they get their hands on it. And those professional places must also observe strict rules regarding radiation protection and hazardous waste disposal and the safety of the staff must always come first.

It can happen, that a watch, given away for a service after prior agreement and examination that the luminous paint on the dial and hands will not be replaced, can nevertheless come back with such an act of sacrilege, because during the work on the watch, the luminous paint has fallen apart.

In the end, you have to make up your own mind. There is certainly a difference concerning the originality, when, during a service, defective parts, filthy dials, crumbled luminescent paint with dangerous radioactive particles, even markers and hands are replaced with appropriate parts, ideally from the manufacturer, compared to something tinkered together from whatever was lying around, with allegedly original dials painted on cardboard, and prints, that look like an effort gone wrong with a children's stamping set. Here, we have a real disgusting thing, which we call a 'frankenwatch'.

Of course, replacing parts on vintage watches with something original is highly difficult, if not impossible, but in the end: *the movement is the main part of a watch, not the dial and hands!*

If a professional polishing of a stainless-steel case would make things worse in view of originality, it is something I would tend to understand if we are dealing with a watch of Elvis, which was scratched on stage during his last performance of the Jailhouse Rock or if it's a family heritage. But beware! Such 'practical' thinking could in the end lead to the unthinkable – the purchase of a modern quartz watch.

WHAT'S LEFT?

What's left of the original dial, the hands, the leather wristband and buckle, the plating of the case, the original parts inside after a service or repair?

Well, when we talk about radium 226 and other substances, the answer is everything – almost completely – with all its risks and dangers, even if the luminous effect is gone on dial and hands. The reduced effectiveness is, as already mentioned, more connected to the aging process of the zinc-sulfide and the luminous paint as a whole.

A half-life period of 1.600 years for radium, means 50% is gone after 1600 years, and another 50% of the remains (25% of the initial amount) after another 1.600 years and so on. If applied 80 years ago, that means 97.5% left (50% gone in 1600 years = 5% in 160 years and 2.5% in 80 years).

The rest has not disappeared into nowhere but is also still around in the form of other radioactive products in the following decay chain for a very, very long time thereafter, save some of the radon 222, which might have gotten out of the bond and through a few leaks.

In the case of tritium with its short half-life, it's more restricted. Here, things also go a lot faster, with a half-life period of only 12.3 years. The next (and also immediately the last) product in the decay chain, the helium isotope ^3H is stable and not radioactive anymore. Tritium is however a gas, which has its own problematic features in this respect.

To sum up: Dial and hands are not glowing anymore, but all radioactive substances are still there unless the particles have already fallen out at whatever occasion, hopefully not picked up from the workbench by the fingers and digested with the next pizza.

CONCLUSION

Collecting vintage watches with lumed paint on dial and hands is not an unsafe or harmful hobby per se – one must just be careful, especially when opening the watch or even working on it.

There is a constantly growing number of research papers, not dealing with the matter in theory, but based on 'real' examples of radium-lumed timepieces. Individual watches or entire collections are measured and results compared to the limit values for health-endangering radioactive emissions, not too seldom with alarming results. Basing research not only on theory, periodic tables, decay chains or numbers, and reactions from the schoolbooks, but on real radium-lumed watches, provides also the possibility to further differentiate things, but here, we have the first problem: This should all go hand in hand with horological experts!

A scientist *without* any advanced understanding of watches will most likely not come up with sensible assertions and, vice versa, a watchmaker or an advanced collector *without* a good understanding of the underlying scientific issues will normally also not come up with something very meaningful. Of course, I am referring to higher-level research and not a more general summary of the issues.

When measuring radiation, you must know something about the different types of cases and housings, not just how to take things apart and back together in the right fashion. We have primitive two-shell cases, screw-backs, snap-backs up to the 'front-loaders', which open up only through the front by removing the crystal with a very effective enclosure of the movement and dial. There are waterproof watches up to the divers, and constructions of crown and stems, firmly sealed (when new), down to some 1930s /1940s watches, open like a barn door in this respect.

I could list many other things here, which, altogether, would make large differences concerning the testing objects and the subsequent results.

Emissions coming from a radium lumed watch lying in a drawer are one thing (dangerous enough), but we also want to know what happens when the watch is opened. With the crystal still on the watch, you can't even measure the alpha-radiation, which can already be shielded off by a piece of paper.

An acrylic watch crystal (also glass of course) will shield off alpha-radiation and the stainless-steel case will shield off beta-radiation from the wrist. But the overall condition can change. What, if the watch crystal has become fragile (often hardly visible) or is already full of cracks? The seals might have suffered fatigue and break and the luminescent paint has degenerated over time, partly crumbled to dust, and is falling around inside the watch?

It is a common perception now, that the storage alone of radium-lumed watches (especially in larger amounts) can be dangerous in unventilated rooms and scientific findings are nowadays accompanied by statements like 'the readings indicated significantly higher than expected radioactive concentrations'.

Tests are performed under real conditions, with or without ventilation, and simulating the domestic environment of a typical collector. However, some tests had been immediately interrupted, due to observation of 'hazardous conditions' in conflict with workplace-safety laws, thus creating the need for a different set-up and place, whilst the conclusions were occasionally drifting away again to 'hypothetical rooms'.

So, whilst the scientists are more and more concerned about safety measures in the testing process to minimize the health risks coming from the radioactive material, some watch collectors are taking the watch apart and tinker around, without a clue about the dangers. Whatever you think about that, it just doesn't fit together – one way or the other.

Measurements of randomly chosen collections as a whole are still predominant, but large individual differences have at least been noted. If you would do the research based on a much larger number of individual watches, one would most likely see, that the present findings are more a sweeping synopsis in a fashion theme, especially when it comes to the dangers of radon.

In the end, you must also do this for each watch separately, although the overall measurement is not equal to the total of all individual readings due to certain properties in an aggregation.

Values are of course constantly fluctuating, not only influenced by the background radiation. The decay in the decay chain is an ongoing process of reducing and increasing volumes between the isotopes.

Some of this research seems like fishing in murky waters.

Measuring radiation is one thing, but you should also deal with what you have, besides radium and its followers in the decay chain. What about strontium or promethium for instance?

And then, the other way around, you should also not let yourself be fooled by belittlements or comparisons relating individual doses to the annual burden or radioactivity around us. To contribute to some enlightenment in this respect, let me give an – admittedly drastic – example:

Let's say, we measure a blow to the head in bumps (Bu). A light bump, like a slap on the forehead, would be valued at 0.1 Bu. A firmer blow, after someone has noticed that he forgot the end of an eBay auction for a vintage watch he always wanted to have, would be estimated at 0.3 Bu. From here upwards, a real knock on the head, perhaps from a hard ball flying towards a person, an acquaintance with the bathroom cabinet, a meeting with a light pole, the windshield etc., up to severe craniocerebral traumas caused by whatever, and finally the lethal blow with a baseball bat, valued as 1.0 Bu.

If the severest can be excluded, all the lighter incidents might all add up to, let's say, 300 Bu annually.

And then, someone comes along and tells you that this lethal blow with the baseball bat of 1.0 Bu on someone's head can't be so bad. After all, it's just 0.33% of the annual dose of 300 Bu or a mere 0.18% of the 547.5 Bu which are already accumulated annually, just by more firmly hitting the forehead five times a day, because someone is so forgetful.

No danger at all, never – radioactivity is largely harmless! Really?

Whatever, the prime danger comes from getting the stuff *inside* the body, by inhaling or digestion. As an additional source of danger, we have the possible inhaling of radon 222. The serious physical damage comes with a delay, often years. Already smallest portions can cause harm, individually or in a cumulative process.

As usual, especially if 'certain interests' must be protected, there is a wide range of opinions, from scaremongering to totally harmless – remember: radium was once considered to be healthy – the more you drank, the more you applied, the better ...

With so much dispute amongst watch collectors and, for that matter, also between professionals in this field, you have to come to your own judgement. You can refer to specialist articles, but you should have at least a basic understanding about what's going on and why.

It cannot be repeated often enough: Radioactive radiation can't be perceived with our sensory organs, you can't see radioactivity or feel it immediately (the latter in relation to the type and amount of radiation we are talking about), but it can cause harm in our body, commonly referred to as biological effects: immediate damages (acute radiation injury) or those, which can be felt only after several years (late damages/late effects) or even genetic damages (hereditary defects), which show up later in the progeny.

Before you shield off the room containing your vintage watch collection from the rest of the house and take care for ventilation five times a day, you should also look for many other items around, like certain ceramics made until the 1970s (glazes colored with radionuclides), canary glass (uranium for the yellow-green color glowing bright green under black light), cloisonné jewelry (uranium in the glaze), older camera lenses from the 1950s to the 1970s (thorium incorporated into the glass) and what have you. Get rid of your old television in the garage with its CRTs (cathode ray tubes emitting x-rays) and do not tamper with your smoke detector to avoid getting in conflict with the radioactive americium 241.

Lastly, a study of the postal laws of the country, referring to the dispatch of radioactive goods (to a lesser extend individual watches, but to a bunch of lumed hands etc.) could be advisable. Watchmakers (but also some watch collectors) should also look at the legal provisions regarding the storage of radioactive goods of certain types and in certain quantities.

US Radium Corporation, view into an old room in the
paint application section on the second floor

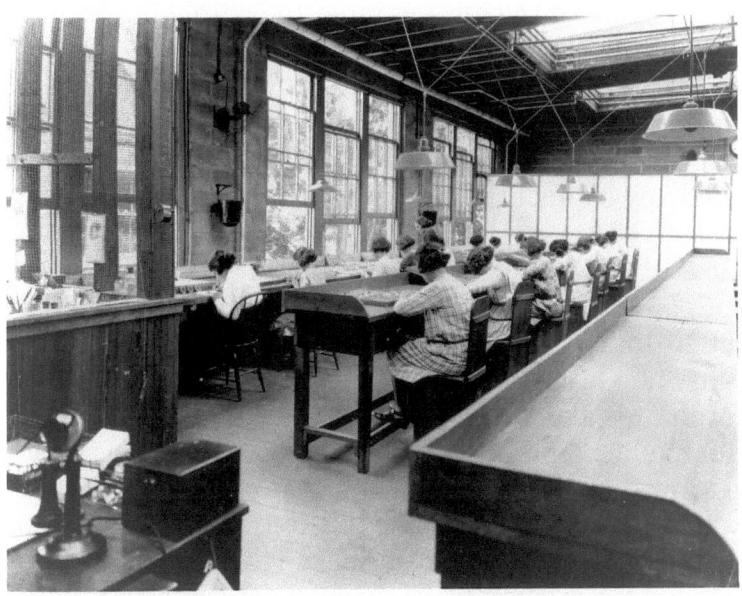

The Radium Girls, workers at the factory of the
US Radium Corporation

69

THE RADIUM GIRLS

Numerous articles and books have been written about the Radium Girls; therefore, I should restrict myself to a few words. The Radium Girls were amongst the first, later very prominent victims and examples of radium poisoning in an industrial process. The way the harmful substance found its way into the body was by ingestion.

The United States Radium Company (formerly Radium Luminous Material Corporation) was extracting and purifying radium from Carnotite ore and used it to produce luminous paint for watch dials and instruments, brought to the market under the name 'UNDARK'. It was applied in their plant in New Jersey by female workers, under the assumption and even confirmation by the company, that the paint used was harmless. They were even instructed to frequently point their brushes with the lips to get finer lines or dots. Other and safer methods were considered to be too time-consuming. For the fun of it, some of the girls painted their fingernails and even teeth with this glowing substance.

The management and scientists of the company were – at least to a good extend – already aware of the dangers and had avoided any contact themselves.

Many of the women later suffered from anemia, bone fractures, and necrosis of the jaw. The company was very reluctant to admit any guilt or responsibility and attributed the illness to other causes, thereby sinking to the lowest level of corporate- and human behavior. Guided by their lawyers and embedded into a slow-moving court system, they used disgusting delaying tactics in an attempt to postpone the trial until the possible death of the women, but in the end, public outcry, instigated by the press, kicked the right asses and even influenced the moving up of the trial date.

The management, along with their shysters, sunk so low, that they could have shaken hands with lower forms of life. They even had the guts to tell the public that they are just facing the consequences of their good-naturedness, because they had employed girls in frail health, along with other intentionally misleading statements, bringing worried workers back to the job under unchanged conditions.

But to top this all by attributing things to other causes, like syphilis, thereby also – in full awareness of the facts – attempting to ruin the reputations of the girls and to suggest a loose living style of the victims in view of the pending legal proceedings, is a behavior way below any ethical standards of the human race and one of the lowest points on the downwardly open scale of crooked legal representation.

At last, over time and occasionally interrupting the Sleeping Beauty slumber of the courts, some damages were finally paid in 1938.

Even the medical sector became part of the evil game by not releasing relevant data to the public, pushed to do so by the company.

The inventor of the radium dial paint, Dr. Sabin A. Von Sochocky, became a victim of radium poisoning himself and later helped the girls in court. He died in 1928.

During these days, between WWI and WWII and beyond, the military continued to be the driving force in need for radioluminescent dials on watches and instruments and dangers to life and health from radium-contaminated paint were the least problems. It took some time to generally realize the real effects coming from radium, or better radioactivity as such. After the first nuclear tests, people were unsuspectingly walking around at the site and inspecting it, after the place had cooled off.

In the 1920s, the drinking of radium-infused water was even seen as healthy. A product called 'RADITHOR', a 'certified' drink, consisting of distilled water mixed with radium 26 and radium 228, developed by a college dropout, was advertised (and heavily consumed during 1918 and 1931) as promoting health, a cure for several diseases, a 'perpetual sunshine', along with other weird statements.

It took a fatal disease of a wealthy American industrialist and member of the High Society to finally make the public understand what's going on and to raise the right interest in the matter. Eben Byers drank some liters of Radiathor on a daily basis, following an injury. This was suggested to him by a real medical doctor. He finally died from radium poisoning in 1932. Based on his popularity, also as a golfer (American amateur champion 1906), things were more intensively discussed and dealt with, compared to the case of the Radium Girls, with their reputation cunningly spoiled by the shysters and their clients.

'Healthy' radium was everywhere, in cosmetic products, for instance in *'Radium and Beauty'* made by Radior Toilet Requisites Ltd., *the first toilet preparations to embody actual radium*, with numerous other magic bullets around. Radium could be found in cotton, sold in France as *'le meilleur des cotons a repriser'* (the best darning cottons). The list of materials contaminated with radium for the sake and well-being of humans would be endless.

At some stage and after the problems became too obvious to be neglected, the public opinion changed, which finally led to a strengthening of the US Food and Drug Administration, but they did not have to take Radithor off the market anymore. Because of the many articles in the press, mainly around the illness and final death of Eben Byers, the company itself had already done this.

The highly regarded Wall Street Journal, traditionally more embedded in the world of financial locusts and -sharks, came out with the headline of the Eben Byers story in best tabloid press style: *'The radium water had worked fine until his jaws came off'*.

Eben Byers was buried in a lead-lined coffin and when exhumed in 1965 for studies, his remains were still highly radioactive.

Before the hard-core vintage watch collectors, especially those keen on lumed timepieces from the 1940s and 1950s, are now tempted to include appropriate precautions in their testimony, they should be informed, that he drank about 1400 bottles of 'Radithor', in total three times the lethal dose.

Whatever, the historical impact of the story of the Radium Girls (and of course Eben Byers) was enormous and occupies an important place, both in the field of health physics and labor rights movement, including the right for individuals to sue for damages from corporations. Industrial safety standards were largely enhanced.

The scientific impact was also important. The Center for Human Radiobiology was established at the Argonne National Laboratory in the USA, providing medical examinations for the surviving radium dial painters, with subsequent evaluations for the benefit of all.

Also available, the book generally dealing with collecting vintage watches:

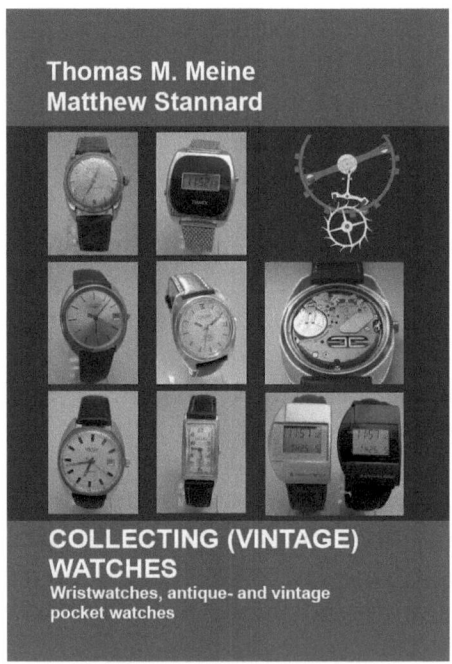

Thomas M. Meine
Matthew Stannard

COLLECTING (VINTAGE)
WATCHES
Wristwatches, antique- and vintage
pocket watches

ISBN: 9 783744 894920